NUMEROLOGY FOR CAREER GUIDANCE

Embrace Wisdom, Unlock Hidden

Opportunities, Overcome Challenges,

and Live a Purposeful & Fulfilling Life.

DR. ARUN KUMAAR KHANDA

https://arunkumarrk.com

Acknowledgments:

In my journey as an author, I have been blessed with support that has significantly contributed to my success. I am deeply grateful to my mentor and bestselling author, Mr. Som Bathla, for his mentorship, motivation, and guidance in writing, self-publishing, and launching my books, which has been crucial on my path to becoming an author-entrepreneur.

I also extend my heartfelt thanks to my author community, especially to Sooraj Achar, a bestselling author himself, for his timely technical support, encouragement, and invaluable advice, which have made my work much easier.

My gratitude goes out to my readers for their unwavering support. I am also thankful for this incredible platform that provides authors with the resources needed to transform the lives of millions.

Thank you all for being a part of this journey. Readers can connect with me at akkhanda9@gmail.com.

Sincerely,

Arun Kumaar Khanda

TABLE OF CONTENTS

Why to Read this Book?............................11

Key Takeaways............................12

Chapter 1............................19

What is Numerology?

Chapter 2............................29

The Basic Concepts

Preparation of Numeroscope

Chapter3............................42

Compatibility of Numbers.

Chapter 4............................57

Friendly and Non-friendly Color

Chapter 5............................66

Numbers Speak the Professions

Chapter6............................70

Detection of Professions from Numeroscope

Chapter7..76

Big Arrow and Small Arrow

Conclusion..82

Disclaimer..89

May I Ask You For a Small Favor?....................90

WHY TO READ THIS BOOK?

- Unlock hidden potential and discover your strengths through numerology.

- Gain clarity on your ideal career path based on your birth numbers.

- Learn how numbers influence your success, decisions, and opportunities.

- Align your personal energies with the right profession for prosperity.

- Overcome challenges and seize opportunities with confidence.

- Empower yourself to make informed, strategic career choices.

- Experience personal growth and professional transformation through self-awareness.

KEY TAKEAWAYS

Chapter one

Numerology as a Life Guide:

Numerology is the science of numbers that uncovers hidden vibrational energy, that influences our destiny from birth to death. The text emphasizes that numbers are inseparable from life, and by harnessing their power, individuals can transform their future, reduce struggles, and gain self-awareness.

Career Alignment Through Numerology:

The book addresses the misalignment many people face in their careers due to family pressure, immediate financial needs, lack of self-awareness, or proper guidance. By using tools like Moolanka, Bhagyanka, and the Lo-Shu Grid, individuals can discover the right career path that aligns with their birth chart and personal strengths.

Empowerment Through Knowledge and Remedies:

The text emphasizes that every problem in numerology has a solution. By diagnosing weaknesses in one's numeroscope, understanding compatible numbers and colors can significantly improve one's success and well-being, empowering individuals and those around them.

Chapter Two

Understanding the Lo-Shu Grid:

_The Lo-Shu Grid is central to numerology, with its 3x3 structure filled with numbers 1-9, where each row, column, and diagonal adds up to 15. This Grid also called the Laxmi Yantra in India, is used to analyze personality traits, strengths, and weaknesses based on the arrangement of numbers. It offers insight into a person's fortune and life journey through different yoga formed by these lines.

Moolanka, Bhagyanka, and Kua Number:

These three numbers—Moolanka (root number), Bhagyanka (destiny number), and Kua number—are critical in numerology. Moolanka is derived from the day of birth, Bhagyanka is the sum of the entire birth date, and Kua number is based on the birth year, calculated differently for males and females. These numbers provide a roadmap for understanding a person's life path and destiny.

Creating a Numeroscope:

The Numeroscope, prepared using the Lo-Shu Grid, Moolanka, Bhagyanka, and Kua numbers, helps in mapping out an individual's numerological profile. The chapter illustrates how to calculate these numbers and fill the grid through examples, highlighting how repeated numbers and empty blocks can indicate strengths and weaknesses in an individual's chart.

Chapter Three

Vibrational Harmony of Numbers:

Each number carries a distinct energy and frequency, symbolized by planetary and mythological associations. Numbers become compatible when their frequencies resonate harmoniously, especially when considering the Moolanka and Bhagyanka.

Role of Friendship, Neutrality, and Enmity:

Numbers exhibit specific relationships categorized as friends, non-friends, and neutral. For instance, number 1 (Sun) forms strong friendships with number 9 (Mars) and number 2 (Moon), reflecting a hierarchical bond between a king, commander, and queen. On the other hand, enmity exists between number 1 and number 8 (Saturn) due to a mythological feud.

Complex Interplay in Permanent vs. Temporary Relationships:

The compatibility of numbers can vary based on the duration of their interaction. Numbers like 4 and 8 may be friendly in temporary associations but struggle to maintain harmony in long-term relationships like marriages or business partnerships. This highlights how number dynamics evolve with context.

Chapter Four

Numerology and Color Compatibility:

Colors have a significant influence on emotions, actions, and personality traits. In numerology, determining your favorable and non-favorable colors depends on the compatibility between your Moolanka (Root Number) and Bhagyanka (Destiny Number). The friendly or non-friendly numbers to both Moolanka and Bhagyanka define which colors will bring you luck and success.

Color Symbolism and Personality:

Each color carries specific meanings and influences, such as red symbolizing leadership and passion. Green represents growth and prosperity, and white denotes spirituality and calmness. Understanding the symbolism behind colors allows individuals to harness their energy and select the right colors for different aspects of life.

Practical Use of Color for Success:

Color is a powerful tool that can be applied in daily life to influence mood and success. Whether through clothing, home decor, vehicles, or other personal belongings, selecting colors that align with your favorable numbers can enhance your well-being and overall fortune.

Chapter Five

Each Number Aligns with Specific Professions:

In numerology, every number is linked to a planet, which influences the types of professions that best suit individuals. For instance, number 1 (Sun) aligns with leadership roles in politics or administration, while number 3 (Jupiter) is associated with knowledge and education-related careers like teaching and counseling.

Planetary Influence Determines Career Paths:

The nature of the planet governing a number dictates the recommended profession. For example, number 6 (Venus), governed by luxury and glamour, suits professions in the entertainment, fashion, and hospitality industries, while number 8 (Saturn), symbolizing discipline and justice, aligns with careers in law, judiciary, and manufacturing.

Numeroscope Offers Deeper Insights:

This chapter provides general career suggestions based on Moolanka (Root Number). However, a more personalized and precise professional prediction can be obtained through a detailed analysis of one's numeroscope, which considers multiple factors beyond just the Moolanka.

Chapter Six

Moolanka and Bhagyanka Play a Key Role:

The core numbers for detecting a profession are the Moolanka (psychic number) and Bhagyanka (lifepath number). These two numbers help identify career paths that align with an individual's strengths, provided they are not anti-numbers (opposing). Profession of Anti-number should be avoided when selecting a profession.

Numeroscope Shows Compatibility for Career Choices:

A numeroscope, by analyzing Moolanka, Bhagyanka, and other key numbers, reveals professions that suit a person's unique traits. For instance, individuals with strong teaching, occult, or research numbers are likely to thrive in those fields, while others may find their luck in banking, law, or sports.

Educational Qualification Matters:

While numerology offers insights into potential career paths, a person's educational background also influences professional selection. For example, someone studying law might find success in the legal field if their numeroscope aligns with those traits, even if other paths could have suited them.

Chapter Seven

Big Arrows Reflect Powerful Traits:

In the Lo-Shu Grid, complete vertical, horizontal, and diagonal lines (Big Arrows) reveal significant characteristics in individuals. For example, people with the vertical line 9-1-5 are natural decision-makers and fighters, while those with the horizontal arrow 8-1-6 possess practical, analytical minds, leading them to prosperity.

Small Arrows Indicate Partial Strengths:

A Small Arrow represents a partially formed line with two numbers. These incomplete lines show specific traits, like 9-7, which gives people the ability to remain calm and balanced in challenging situations, thanks to a combination of fighting spirit (9) and wisdom (7).

Arrows Provide Insight Into Career and Personality:

The presence of certain arrows (Big or Small) can guide predictions about a person's career or life path. For instance, those with diagonal lines like 4-5-6 tend to be aggressive but successful in their endeavors, while individuals with 3-9 may face frequent litigation due to their strong egos and unwillingness to compromise.

Chapter One

WHAT IS NUMEROLOGY?

"Numbers are the building blocks of the universe." - Plato

Welcome to my third book **"NUMEROLOGY FOR CAREER GUIDANCE"** on numerology. I hope you are more or less familiar with the concept and scope of numerology. Do you know where is the knowledge? Guess now and give some thought to your brilliant working mind. Yes, you are right, knowledge is everywhere. You have to give a little bit of patience and interest to acquire it. Knowledge can be acquired from teachers, mentors, parents, seniors, books, etc. It is acquired for self-upliftment, knowledge, progress, empowerment, winning, and achieving dreams. It is also for sharing for the expansion of knowledge fostering growth, innovation, and understanding. **Dānena na kṣīyate vidyā ratnaṁ mahādhanam.**

Numerology is a concept that believes in the vibrational energy of each number. It is a science of numbers. The exploration of hidden energy kept in numbers is the basic concept in numerology. You may not be aware but the numbers are following you from time immemorial. You found this book indicates that you are curious to know about yourself with the magic of numbers and believe in the cycle of death and birth. There is a focused verse in Sanskrit attributed to Adi Shankaracharya;

पुनरपि जननं पुनरपि मरणं

पुनरपि जननी जठरे शयनम्।

punarapi jananaṁ punarapi maraṇaṁ

punarapi jananī jaṭhare śayanaṁ।

The above verse highlights that being a living being you are destined to pass through the endless cycle of birth and death unless you know the art to get salvation. To make your future secure you need to take the corrective actions today.

As you sow so you reap. You may not ignore or deny this fact. The struggle or the achievements you are enjoying are the result of your previous incarnations. Your belief system is not an exception to it. Like astrology numerology is the product of our belief system, which evolved thousands of years ago. As successor, we are taking forward its legacy nothing more, and trying to inhale the nectar out of it for our progress and fulfillment.

NUMBERS ARE PART AND PARCEL OF YOUR LIFE.

Numbers are present everywhere. Hans Decoz says;

"Numbers are the language of the universe, and through numerology, we can understand the deeper meanings of our lives."

I can tell you with authority that no one including you can deny the presence of numbers in their lives. Because from your birth to your death, for every incarnation, numbers are with you. It will remain with you for an indefinite period till you get solvation. Numbers and you appear to be inseparable. It is like two sides of a coin. When you try to separate two sides you will lose the coin and its values. Remember numbers are the language of the universe and you are the product of the universe. How can numbers leave you alone? We have to find the energy possessed by numbers and harness them for our optimum benefits.

Nine numbers starting from 1 to 9 are used to calculate the destiny of an individual in numerology. Zero is never used in numerology, unlike mathematics.

1 is the number that represents the SUN.

2 is the number that represents the MOON.

3 is the number that represents JUPITER.

4 is the number that represents RAHU

5 is the number that represents MERCURY.

6 is the number that represents VENUS.

7 is the number that represents KETU.

 8 is the number that represents SATURN.

9 is the number that represents MARS.

In astrology, you can find all of the above planets and their effects on the horoscope. But in numerology, we use numbers to predict the future. Some numbers are friends to each other and some treat each other as enemies. Some numbers behave neutrally. It is just like human behavior. As you see in our social scenario, some behave friendly some act like enemies and few don't care about our cause, the same principles apply in numerology. Why? Because we all are connected to the same energy source, some say that is infinite intelligence. We all are there in one photo frame.

HAVE YOU EVER THOUGHT YOUR DATE OF BIRTH IS SPECIAL?

Have you ever thought that you are unique and the secret is hiding in your date of birth? If you have not treated yourself special to date, you have done injustice to yourself.

"Love yourself first, and everything else falls into line." - Camila Cabello

From now start loving yourself. It is called self-love, the unique one where you may not have to pay anything but to attend to yourself. You might have faced obstacles and setbacks in your life. Might have been disappointed with your fortune. You might have visited the astrologers but in vain. Believe me, the secret is there in your date of birth. No date of birth is good or bad. God has given enough to you, but you could not find the diamond from it. Don't worry I will tell you the secret of your date of birth. Find out the best from it for your transformation. It will definitely reduce your struggle. Give a big smile on your face and increase your happiness and well-being.

Let you try the concept of numerology in your life and see what happens. Knowledge is everywhere in the books, in our teachers, and on the internet. But unless you know the way to utilize it for excellence, the same knowledge is useless for you.

Let me tell you some of the secrets of your date of birth. In every date of birth, there are 81 combinations of MOOLANKA and BHAGYANKA. They indicate your life path and direction. I have discussed it in my first book "UNLOCK YOUR DESTINY WITH NUMEROLOGY" in detail.

When we prepare a Numeroscope or birth chart from your date of birth, you cannot find the presence of all the 9 numbers, unlike a horoscope. You can find some numbers are present and some are missing from the date of birth. It is said out of one million one birth chat can witness the presence of all 9 numbers in the chart. It is definitely the rarest of rare events.

You can find eight types of lines and eight types of Yogas in the Lo-Shu Grid. From the grid, we find the strengths and weaknesses of the individual. Now you can ask how you can find the hidden treasure from the chart. How can you overcome the weakness of your birth chart?

Numerology can explain everything you want to know.

You can find the missing numbers from your date of birth. The missing numbers indicate you are missing something in your life. But nothing to worry about. Every problem has a solution.

"Every problem has a solution; it may sometimes just need another perspective." -Katherine Russell

Yes, I have answers to all your questions. When diagnosis is made, then treatment is easy. We can do remedies for the missing numbers. Believe me, you are unique and the remedies will make you unstoppable. You can explore your strengths and overcome your weaknesses without much expenditure and effort. My second book "NUMEROLOGY: A PRACTICAL GUIDE" is the answer to the above issues.

Can you imagine your name spelling may foil your plan if not done according to your birth chart? Have you ever heard before that mere name spelling can change your fortune?

Yes, different case studies suggest that 30-40% of your success or failure depends on your name spelling. If your name spelling is corrected according to your birth date you may get 30-40% more success in your life. I myself have corrected my name spelling and getting the benefit.

Further, we can predict your future years, months, and dates. Future predictions can help you to make better decisions for better predictions in your life.

WHAT IS THERE FOR YOU IN THIS BOOK?

Many of us are in the wrong boat in choosing our professions. Many surveys and studies found the above truth. But why we are in the wrong boat? The reason may be many.

> - **Family background:** For example, a family of bureaucrats wishes their sons or daughters to follow in their footprints, even as the children are interested in other professions like painting, acting, healing, etc.

> - **Immediate needs of the family**: The earning member of the family died untimely and no option left for the

survival of the family. Now the man is left to embrace any profession to earn money to feed the family.

➢ **Lack of self-awareness:** One is not aware of his own talent and chooses to right profession.

➢ **Lack of proper guidance**: A burning desire leads you to a logical conclusion about your true value and goals. Lack of burning desires lands you in the wrong professions.

What are the consequences of wrong professions?

- The lack of job satisfaction.

- Misalignments with skills and interests.

- Unhappy from within.

- May feel inferior to his friends who got better opportunities even being less talented.

- May face challenges in family life.

But don't worry. This book will guide you in selecting the right profession as per your birth chart. Here you will get the basic knowledge to prepare your own numeroscope. Get familiar with the lo-Shu grid, moolanka, Bhagyanka, and Kua number, the basic information for the preparation of your birth chart. Compatibility of numbers, friendly and non-friendly colors are discussed for your empowerment. It also discusses the professions associated with different numbers and how to detect the right professions from your birth chart.

The beauty of numerology is it only needs a date of birth, no day, time, or place of birth is required, unlike astrology.

You can implement the science of numerology in your life for your perfection. Remember no one is perfect on this planet. Everyone has the scope to improve. Capacity building and acquiring knowledge give anyone more power. You can use it for the improvement of your family members like your parents, wife/husband, children, friends, and relatives. Can you imagine a small piece of advice that may do wonders in anyone's life? Can put a smile on the lips of many. Then why not implement it? Remember, learning is a continuous process and empowerment is your choice.

Summary:

This book, "Numerology for Career Guidance," introduces readers to the significance of numerology in understanding themselves and shaping their future. The chapter emphasizes that knowledge is omnipresent and accessible through effort and curiosity. It highlights the unique vibrational energies associated with numbers and how they influence every aspect of life, from birth to death. This chapter explains that numbers, like planetary influences, shape destinies of the individual, and interpersonal relationships.

The numerology revolves around nine key numbers, each representing a celestial body. These numbers guide the calculation of an individual's destiny and career path. The chapter explains how numerology differs from astrology by relying solely on the birth date, rather than the time or place of birth. Missing numbers in one's numeroscope indicate areas of weakness that can be addressed through specific remedies.

The book promises to help readers discover their strengths, overcome weaknesses, and choose careers aligned with their true potential. The readers can unlock hidden opportunities and enhance their success by understanding the energies of numbers and their personal birth charts,

Chapter Two

THE BASIC CONCEPTS

"Numerology, like astrology, predicts future trends and patterns by analyzing the numbers in your life." — Anonymous

LO-SHUGRID

I feel you are more or less aware of the basic structure of the numeroscope called the **Lo-Shu Grid.**

4	9	2
3	5	7
8	1	6

The above image filled with numbers is called the Lo-Shu Grid. It is also called LAXMI YANTRA in India.

As you see it has 9 blocks in 3x3 grid format. Each block is represented with one number from 1-9. You can see that the grid has 3 vertical, 3 horizontal, and two diagonal lines. All the lines form separate **Yoga** in numerology. But the grid is formed so intelligently and scientifically that if you count the numbers in any line, you will find a total of 15. Isn't it amazing? All the credit goes to Lo-Shu, the creator of the grid. Further, if you add 1 and 5(15), you will get 6. Number 6 represents Venus, the planet of luxury, success, and glamor. Each line bears a specific name and represents the specific characteristics. We will learn each and every aspect of the line, their importance, and their implications on the birth chart. We can learn how these lines can make or break our fortune, personality traits, etc.

You will find it very interesting on your journey to know more as proceed further. Numerology is a hope for everyone. You will find out why some people are so successful and why others are not. Do you know what the basic difference between a successful and an unsuccessful is? It is deciphering the Numeroscope. The proper analysis of the birth chart can make you unstoppable and overcome weakness.

Be optimistic and happy. Many more things will follow for your empowerment in the next chapters.

The Lo-Shu grid concept comes from Chinese numerology. Are you excited to know why such name Lo-Shu Grid is given to the particular number structure? Let me explain to you the legend behind it.

The Lo Shu Grid gets its name from the Luo River (Lo-Shu in pinyin) near Luoyang, Henan in China. Legend says a giant turtle (sometimes referred to as a "divine turtle") emerged from the Yellow River carrying the Lo Shu grid pattern on its back.

According to legend, the Lo Shu Square, a 3x3 magic square where the numbers 1 to 9 are arranged such that the sum of the numbers in each row, column, and diagonal equals 15, was revealed to Saint Lo-Shu by a turtle. This event was seen as a sign of good fortune, and the pattern was named after Saint Lo-Shu, who had seen the grid first on the back of the tortoise

<u>MOOLANKA, BHAGYANKA & KUA NUMBER</u>.

What are **MOOLANKA** (root number), **BHAGYANKA** (destiny number), and **Kua Number**? These three terminologies are important elements in numerology and preparation of your birth chart. How can you find these numbers from your date of birth? In the first instance, it appears to be difficult, but as you progress further it appears very easy. I was also facing such a type of insecurity in my mind. Without taking an example it can't be explained.

Let us take an example of the **date of birth of Raj is 13th November 1962.**

Moolanka:

In the instance case, Moolanka of Raj is 4. You may ask how it is calculated. It is very simple. Just add the birth date. In this case, the birth date was 13. When we add 1 with 3(1+3=4) got four. If the birth date is a single digit like 1,2,3 ......9, it is treated as moolanka without any addition. For example, if the birth date is 29, then what would be the moolanka? When you add 2 with 9(2+9=11) you will get 11 and if reduced to a single digit you will get 2(1+1=2). Now we got the moolanka as 2.

Bhagyanka:

It is also easy to find out bhaghanka. When the numbers of the entire date of birth, date, month, and year are added together we get the bhagyanka. In the case of Raj birth date(13) +Month(11)+Year(1962). The next step is to add all the numbers and reduce them to a single digit i,e. 1+3+1+1+1+9+6+2=25=2+5=7. Now we got the Bhagyanka of Raj as 7.

Kua Number:

Now the next and third important number left is called **(PA)KUA NUMBER**. Calculation of this number from a date of birth is a little bit interesting. Because its calculation is different in the case of males and females. Here only birth year is needed for calculation. Let us calculate. Take the birth year of X Raj. It is 1962. The addition of the total numbers 1+9+6+2 comes to 18 or 1+8=9. Consider Raj as a male and his Kua number can be calculated as **11-9=2.**

Now **KUA NUMBER OF Raj** comes to 2. But you may ask why the sum total of the birth year is subtracted from 11. The answer is it is a formula. Follow the principle "PUT THE FORMULA AND GET THE ANSWER."

Now it is the turn of a female. Let a **female Y** born in the year 1962. We can calculate the Kua number of Y by adding 4 to the sum total of birth year. Her birth year total is (1+9+6+2=18=1+8=9) is 9. Now **KUA NUMBER OF Y** shall be **9+4=13=4**

Now I am confident that you are comfortable in calculating the Kua number in the case of male and female. In the instance case, Kua number of Raj(male) comes to **2,** and Kua number of Y(Female) comes to **4.**

In some circumstances, you can find both the bhagyanka and moolanka are the same. Thanks for your interest in this topic. Let us move further to understand how to prepare a Numeroscope.

PREPARATION OF NUMEROSCOPE

NUMEROSCOPE

LO-SHU GRID

An astrologer prepares a horoscope from a date, place, and time of birth. Numerologists prepare a Numeroscope from date of birth only. For the preparation of a birth chart or Numeroscope, the Lo-Shu grid is considered a guiding compass. Now look at the Lo-Shu Grid Lend the position of the number in the grid. See carefully the 9 blocks and the position of the numbers. Take a piece of paper and prepare a grid on it from your date of birth as per the numeroscope.

Consider the **date of birth of X is 13.08. 1967.**

In this instance case, the birth date of X is 13. As said in numerology, we have to add a double-digit number to a single digit. Now when we add (1+3) we can get 4. Now the Moolanka of X comes to **4.**

Now proceed to the second number the **bhagyanka.** Now how can we calculate the bhagyanka? It is very simple and illustrated above. However, once again for your practice, I am to say that it is the total sum of X's birth date, month, and year. In this case, the date is 13, the month is 8, and the year is 1967. The total of all the digits comes to (1+3+8+1+9+6+7)35 and the sum of 35 comes to (3+5) 7. Now we get the bhagyanka of X as 7.

You may ask one question if the sum total of a date of birth comes to 10 or 20, what can be considered as the correct number? It is a good question. In numerology 0 is not considered as a number. Hence in the case of 10, it can be said 1, and in place of 20, you can count it as 2.

Another important terminology often used is **PSYCHIC NUMBER** in numerology for MOOLANKA. Similarly, the bhagyanka is often called by the name **DESTINY NUMBER** or **LIFE PATH NUMBER.**

Now the next and third number left is called **(PA)KUA NUMBER**. Calculation of this number from a date of birth is a little bit interesting as calculated in the previous chapter. Because its calculation is different in the case of males and females. Here only birth year is needed for calculation. Let us calculate. Take the birth year of X. It is 1967. The addition of the total numbers 1+9+6+7 comes to 23 or 2+3 =5. Consider X as a male and his Kua number can be calculated as **11-5=6.** Now **KUA NUMBER OF X** comes to 6.

Now it is the turn of a female. Let a **female Y** born in the year 1967. We can calculate the Kua number of Y by adding 4 to the sum total of birth year. Her birth year total is (1+9+6+7=23=2+3) is 5. Now **KUA NUMBER OF Y** shall be **5+4=9.**

Now I am confident that you are comfortable in calculating the Kua number in the case of male and female. In the instance case, Kua number of X(male) comes to **6,** and Kua number of Y(Female) comes to **9**.

Now we have all three important numbers from above.

The date of birth of X is 13.08. 1967.

- **Moolanka is 4**

- **Bhagyanka is 7**

- **Kua number is 6 in the case of males and 9 in the case of females.**

Now fill the numbers in the grid as per the Lo-Shu grid. Place all numbers 1, 3, 8, 1, 9, 6, 7 at the proper place. Now place the Moolanka, bhagyanka, and Kua number accordingly.

However, remember one thing. If your moolanka is coming from one single digit (such as 1 to 9) you need not fill it again. In the above instance, case 4 is the moolanka and needs to be filled in.

Have you prepared the Numeroscope of X? If not prepare it ok. It can take only 5 to 10 minutes for the purpose. Wonderful you have done it. Now see the numeroscope I have prepared. Tally it now with yours.

4	9	
3		77
8	11	66

D-4, C-7, K-6

Now take the examples of two more males named James and Jack

Consider the date of birth of James is 15.02. 1987.

4	9	2
	5	7
8	11	66

James: D-6, C-6, K-4

In this case, moolanka and bhagyanka are the same as 6 and the Kua number is 4. As 1 and 6 are repeating they find their place twice in the grid.

Now consider the date of birth of Jack as **06.01.1987.**

4	9	
	5	7
8	11	6

Jack: D-6, C-5, K-4

What do you observe in this chart? 6 is not repeated as a moolanka, because 6 is a single digit and is already present in the chart.

Let me explain and prepare the Numeroscope of two women. Consider their name as LISA and SARA.

The date of birth of LISA is 10.03.1987

	9	22
3		7
8	11	

LISA: D-1, C-2, K-2

In this birth chart, the moolanka is 1, the bhagyanka is 2, and the Kua number is also 2. As the moolanka is 1 and her date of birth is 10 or say 1, the same number can't be entered again. Further, both the bhagyanka and Kua numbers are the same as 2, and it is not found in the date of birth, 2 is placed twice in the chart.

Now let's talk about the birth chart of SARA. Her date of birth **is 19.03.1987.** Her moolanka, bhagyanka, and Kua numbers are the same as LISA's. Now prepare the birth chart.

	99	**22**
3		**7**
8	**111**	

SARA-D-1, C-2, K-2

Now you see the difference between the two birth charts. In the chart of LISA 1 is coming two times and it is coming three times in respect of SARA. Similarly, 9 is coming once in the case of **LISA** and two times in **SARA**'s chart.

I feel you are now very happy and confident to prepare a Numeroscope without any confusion. Now prepare your Numeroscope along with your family members. It will definitely give you confidence to proceed further. Let me talk about the dimensions of both charts. In the charts not a single line is complete, which indicates that both the numeroscopes are weak and three blocks are blanks. In the subsequent chapters, I will talk about the 81 combinations of moolanka and bhagyanka and their implications on the person.

Summary:

The Lo-Shu Grid is also known as Laxmi Yantra in India. It is a 3x3 grid structure where each block represents a number from 1 to 9. This grid, which was derived from Chinese numerology, has a unique arrangement. The sum of numbers in each row, column, and diagonal equals 15. This magical number represents Venus, the planet of luxury and success. Each line in the grid corresponds to a specific yogas, influencing one's fortune and personality. Understanding these lines is important in decoding how they affect your life and learning to harness their power to your advantage.

Key numerological elements like Moolanka (root number), Bhagyanka (destiny number), and Kua number are derived from your birthdate and are integral to preparing a Numeroscope. For instance, Raj, born on 13th November 1962, has a Moolanka of 4, a Bhagyanka of 7, and a Kua number of 2. Moolanka is found by adding the digits of the birth date, Bhagyanka by adding the entire birthdate, and Kua by applying specific formulas for males and females.

The Lo-Shu Grid is the foundation for preparing a Numeroscope. It can reveal your strengths, weaknesses, and career path. By learning how to calculate these numbers and fill them into the grid, you can prepare your own and your family's Numeroscope, opening doors to greater self-understanding and success.

Chapter Three

COMPATIBILITY OF NUMBERS.

"The universe is a symphony of numbers." - Kepler

Each number bears energy and vibrates at a specific frequency. When the frequencies of numbers match, they are called compatible. This compatibility is considered in respect of Moolanka and Bhagyanka.

CHARACTERISTICS OF NUMBERS

Let us see the characteristics of the numbers from 1 to 9.

1. Number one is the Sun, the source of all energies in the solar system. Sun is king of all planets. Hence 1 is king of all numbers starting from 1 to 9.

2. Number 2 is the moon. Moon bears all the qualities of a queen. Moon is called the queen. Moon is also symbolized as a mother.

3. Number 3 is attributed to Jupiter. Jupiter is the teacher or guru of gods. He is called Devguru, a councilor of gods and councilor of the Sun.

4. Number 4 represents Rahu. Rahu is good for the poor and bad for the rich. He plunders the wealth of the rich and distributes it among the poor. His character resembles a gangster. He is the god of the poor but the enemy of the rich. As he bears only a head without a heart or body, he only thinks from his head. You may not get mercy from number 4. He is a symbol of discipline and organization.

5. Number 5 is mercury. He is treated as the prince in numerology. A king, queen, and prince constitute a royal family.

6. Number 6 is Venus. Venus is guru of Danav. He is a councilor and advisor of Demons. He is the best poet and is creative. This number symbolizes enjoyment, glamor, fashion, money, family, and conjugal relationships.

7. Number 7 represents Ketu. It is the lower part of Rahu known as the shadow planet. He is a powerhouse of wisdom.

Now let me tell you a myth of Rahu and Ketu. The mythological story goes like this. Both Deva (god) and Danav(demon) churn the milk ocean jointly. All the precious items including *Kamadhenu* (The wish-fulfilling divine cow), *Uchhaishravas* (A magnificent white horse), *Airavata* (A celestial white elephant), *Kaustubha* (A precious gem),

Parijata (A divine flowering tree), *Varuni* (The goddess of wine), *Apsaras* (Celestial nymphs), *Chandra* (The moon), *Dhanvantari* (The divine physician), *Lakshmi* (The goddess of wealth and prosperity), evolved from it taken away by gods and Rishis, leaving none for the demons, although both have contributed for the purpose. Lastly, *Amrit* came out of the ocean. Lord Vishnu in the guise of a beautiful woman distributed it to the gods. However, in the guise of God Rahu has eaten the nectar. When Vishnu realized the presence of Rahu, he chopped the head making two separate parts by his *Sudarsan Chakra*(discus). As Rahu consumed the nectar did not die and both parts remained alive.

The character of Ketu is that he can't think from his head due to its absence. He does think from the heart. He speaks the language of the associated number. In the other language, if he is fitted with the head of the sun, he acts like a king. If he is fitted with the head of Rahu he gets its complete form. He can behave as per the head he is likely to get.

1. Number 8 is the number of Saturn, the god of justice. He judges himself. He gives awards, rewards, or punishment according to your karma(actions). Have you seen judges in the judiciary system?

They only pronounce the order based on the available facts, documents, arguments, and written submissions produced before them. They have no friends or enemies. They are supposed to be neutral.

9. This number represents Mars. He is treated as a commander and warrior but pious. Purely vegetarian and saint-like.

Now you have a glimpse of the characteristics of the numbers. But we are not aware how they can behave if come together. It is a real game the compatibility of numbers.

COMPATIBILITY OF NUMBERS

Every number has some friends, non-friends, and neutral numbers. Let me draw a table for better appreciation.

Number	Friends	Non-Friends	Neutral
1	9,2,5,3,6,1	8	4,7
2	1,5,3,2	8,4,9	6,7
3	1,5,3,2,7*	6	4,8,9,7*
4	7,1,5,6,4*,8*	4*,8*,2,9	3
5	1,2,3,6,5	....	7,8,9,4
6	1,5,7,6	3	8,9,2,4
7	4,6,1,3,5	....	2,8,9,7
8	5,6,3,7,4*,8*	(4*,8*,)1,2,	9

| 9 | 1,5,3 | 4,2 | 6,7,8,9 |

Let me explain the above chart in detail.

1.

Number 1 represents the sun, the king, who may need only a few's help. The sequence of friends is as follows 9,2,5,3,6,1. You can say it is the king's number. It is royal in his approach and attitude. He runs an empire. What does a king need to run a kingdom, an empire, and keep its territorial integrity? Expand the empire? Annex and conquer the kingdom of the enemy? Can you guess? It is obviously an army or military power. Who is the commander of the military? The answer is no 9, Mars. That is why 1 king is very close to Commander 9. The king can only share some secrets with the commander. It can't even be shared with his beloved wife (queen). Our history witnesses the mutiny of the commanders and chief of armed forces against kings and the seizure of power by army commanders. Now it is clear that the king is nearest to 9.

After number 9, next nearer to number 1 is number 2, the queen. If you want peace in family and marital life, you must love, care, and respect your wife, otherwise, your life will be no less than hell. King is not an exception to it.

Then comes 5, the prince, 3, 6 the councilors, and 1(king) in decreasing orders of priority as shown in the table. You may think how and why 1 is a friend of 1. One answer is self-love and the second answer is foreign relations. A king needs to keep good relations with his counterparts in the neighboring states for peace and prosperity in the region.

Now let's talk about the non-friend column. Here 8, Saturn is the lone enemy of 1, the Sun. Why is Saturn the enemy of the Sun?

There is a myth in Hindu religious scriptures, that Saturn is the illegitimate child of Sun, born to mother Chaya. Sun entered into a relationship with Chaya but did not get her married or recognize her as his wife. The son born to their relationship, Saturn was very dark in complex, for which the sun did not acknowledge him as his son. Saturn demands his recognition as the son of the king, but the sun refuses it, rather than offering a palace, money, property, etc. As the matter was not settled amicably, Saturn maintained his enmity with his father the sun forever.

In a neutral column, you can find 4 and 7. One is gangster and another is headless. A king doesn't need their support at the same time and may not apply his forces against them.

2.

Number 2 is a queen, a wife, and a mother. In the friends list you can see this in 1,5,3,2 sequence. Who comes first as a friend of the queen? It is king, her beloved husband. Can a CHEST WIFE live without her husband? The answer is known to you. After the king, the queen needs her son, the prince of the empire, the future king. Then comes 3, the councilor. In the time of crisis, his advice can save the kingdom. Next comes 2, the queen and her counterparts.

Now see her non-friend's column. Who are they? 8,4,9. First comes 8, Saturn the stepson. A friendly relationship between a stepmother and a stepson may not normally exist. If we see it from a scientific point of view, the moon represents water, and Saturn represents iron. The combination of iron and water makes the iron rust. It is better for them to keep their distance. That is why both 2 and 8 can't stay together in a single column.

4 is a gangster. Queen doesn't like gangsters, and as a woman, one should not like such an unworthy fellow. Next comes number 9, the commander. Queen hates the commander because the king spends most of his time consulting with 9. Further, 9 does not take command from the queen except the king.

Next, come the neutral planets of the moon. Numbers 6 and 7 are neutral to number 2 because the queen rarely needs the advice of Venus. Jupiter is always available to guide the queen as and when necessary. Ketu (7) is headless. How can he support the queen? Number 2 has no enmity or friendship with Ketu. He is left neutral.

3.

Number 3 is Jupiter, the guru of gods. He is pious, vegetarian, and a powerhouse of knowledge. His friends come in the following sequence; 1,5,3,2,7*. He is most friendly with the king. Next comes 5, the prince, the future king as his friend. The next friend of Jupiter is Jupiter himself. Here both are councilors and respect each other. Number 3 has no problem with 2 or queen. Number 7 is the symbol of wisdom. Knowledge and wisdom have a positive equation making them friends.

Number 6 is positioned as a non-friend of number 3. You may ask why. Both 3 and 6 are councilors, both are powerhouses of knowledge. Then why are they non-friends? Because there is a basic difference between the two. 3 is the councilor of gods/devata and 6 is the councilor of demons/danav (Asuras). Both are from different ideologies, as gods and demons are enemies to each other.

Further, 4,8,9,7 are neutral for Jupiter. Because number 3, has no business with 4,8,9,7 (7* may become his friend sometimes due to his wisdom).

4.

Number 4 is Rahu. Can you tell me who would be his best friend? I think you guessed it correctly. It is number 7, Ketu, the lower part of Rahu. The combination of 4 and 7 not only completes the body but also completes the thinking pattern. Number 4 is a good gangster who needs the support of the king to remain in freedom. That is why made friends with 5, the future king. Next comes 6, in his friend list, because both share a common character.

Numbers 2 and 9 are non-friends of 4. Because the queen doesn't need the support of a gangster or believe in him, the characteristics of 9 and 4 are completely different.

Now, 4 and 8 may be friends if their relationship is not permanent. Both may be non-friends if their relationships are made permanent. You are now a little bit confused by the above statement. Am I right? Let me explain. If the people of Moolanka 4 make friends with 4 and 8, then it is okay. But if the simple friendship turns into a permanent relationship in the form of marriage or business partnership, it can't survive.

You find only Jupiter in the neutral column. Gangsters may seek the advice of Jupiter but number 3 keeps a safe distance from it.

5.

Number 5 is Mercury, the prince. The sequence of friends comes as follows 1,2,3,6,5. The prince is closer to his father, the king, and his mother comes second. He has a good rapport with both the councillors 3 and 6. A prince has a good friendship with another prince. Hence 5 is a friend of 5.

It is important to note that a prince has no non-friend. Because when you see the Lo-Shu Grid you can find that 5 is positioned at the center, keeping an equal distance from all the blocks. As a prince 5, maintain neutrality with 7,8,9,4. Similarly, 7,8,9,4 have no problem with the future king 5.

6.

Number 6 is Venus, the guru of demons. He believes in merrymaking, enjoyment, upliftment, progress, fulfillment of needs, and the rise of demons. As a councilor, he is close to the king. Next in closeness come 5, the prince. Number 7, (Ketu) is also his friend because 7 is the disciple of 6. Further, number 6 is the friend of 6, a councilor can be a friend of a councilor.

Number 6 has one non-friend in 3. Because 6 is the guru of demons and 3 is the guru of gods. Both can't see each other, as both are anti-planet. Next, come the neutral numbers in the form of 8,9,2,4. They have no problem with 6.

7.

Number 7 is Ketu. I have told you earlier about the myth behind Ketu. It has no head. Now can you guess who would be his best friend? I feel your presumption is right. It is Rahu, number 4. When 7 is associated with 4 a complete structure is formed, and are made for each other. The next close friend of Ketu is Venus, number 6. Venus is the mentor of 7. They have a relationship of teacher and disciple. Next comes number 1, the king. Being headless he thinks from heart for which he needs the blessings of the king. Jupiter 3, is coming in the queue as the next friend, as Jupiter represents knowledge and 7 represents wisdom. Knowledge is always comfortable with wisdom. Next comes number 5, the prince as the friend of Ketu.

Ketu has no non-friends like Prince Mercury. Now let us see who are the neutral planets for Ketu. They are 8,2,9,7. It is understood that 8, 2, and 9 are neutral for 7, but how and why 7 is neutral for 7? The reason is obvious as 7 is headless and it thinks from the heart. Its thinking is illogical then how an illogical thinker can help another illogical thinker? So, it is better to say 7 is neutral to 7 rather than calling them friends.

8.

Now talk about number 8, Saturn. He administers justice for all. He is a judge and never does injustice to anyone. Have you ever seen the justices of a high court and supreme court? How they maintain neutrality, without much involvement in social gatherings and functions.

Planet Mercury, number 5, is his friend. Number 5 is a prince and a small boy, who may not have any work with a judge, which is why 8 has a friend in his step-brother 5. Other friends of 8 are 6,3,7. Numbers 3 and 6 are persons of knowledge as they are councilors to the king. The judge needs their advice for the administration of justice if needed. Ketu thinks from the heart and may not do any mischief, so he is the friend of 8.

Now see these numbers 4*,8*. ***Relation of 4 and 8 with 8 is friendly when they are occasionally getting together. They are fine in temporary relationships simply as friends. But they may be non-friends if the temporary relationship is further promoted to permanent relationships like marriage, or business partnerships (between 4 & 8, 8 & 8).*** In simple language, I CAN SAY THAT PERMANENT RELATIONSHIPS CAN'T SURVIVE BETWEEN 8 & 8, 8 & 4, AND 4 & 4.

Now you can anticipate who are the enemy or non-friends of Saturn. The number one enemy is the sun, and the second is number 2. Saturn is the illegitimate child of the sun and the sun can't recognize number 8 as his son, for which he always sees the opportunity to take revenge. Moon is the queen and his stepmother. He considers that due to the beauty of his stepmother, his mother is not recognized as a queen of the sun. Furthermore, if we look from a scientific point of view, the moon is water and Saturn is iron. If both the elements come together iron gets rust. They are antiplanets, they should keep away from each other.

Mars, number 9 is the neutral number for 8.

9.

Number 9 is Mars, the warrior the commander. He is unpredictable and a fighter planet. Often driven by mood. His friends include 1,5,3. Being given command in the army he is obliged to king. Next comes 5, the prince, the future king. Number 3, Jupiter is the friend of number 9, because he needs advice from the guru.

Numbers 4 and 2 are non-friends of 9. Rahu is a gangster who can't patch up with the commander. No doubt 2 is queen but 9 doesn't carry out her order. There is a mental war that always runs between the two. More both 4 and 8 are struggling planets. When comes together make the people struggle, struggle, and struggle.

Numbers 6,7,8,9 are neutral planets for number 9. How 9 can be neutral for 9. When a commander meets another commander maintain constraint and avoid confrontation. It is the part of discipline that 9, follows, for which 9 is neutral to nine.

Summary:

This chapter explains the unique characteristics of numbers from 1 to 9 in numerology. Each number speaks about its energies, vibrations, and compatibility with one another. Numbers are connected with celestial bodies and mythological figures. For example, 1 represents the Sun, the king, while 2 represents the Moon, the queen. Each number has friendly, non-friendly, and neutral numbers based on their interactions, similar to human relationships.

Number 1, for instance, is close to 9 (Mars, the commander) and 2 (the queen), but has a tense relationship with 8 (Saturn). Number 5, representing Mercury, the prince, is friendly with all numbers and remains neutral, while 9 (Mars) struggles with 4 (Rahu, the gangster) and 2 (the queen). The chapter also talks about the mythological story of Rahu and Ketu, illustrating the dual nature of these two entities.

Compatibility between numbers is vital in numerology, influencing relationships, partnerships, and destiny. Friendly numbers bring harmony, while non-friendly ones may cause conflict, especially in personal and business relationships. This knowledge empowers us and helps us understand which numbers support or oppose each other, offering a deeper understanding of how numerological energies affect life.

Now this is much toward compatibility of numbers. We will know more further in the subsequent chapters.

Chapter Four

FRIENDLY AND NON-FRIENDLY COLOR

"Colors, like features, follow the changes of the emotions."- Pablo Picasso:

Do you believe the color has any role to play in your life? Have you ever seen a rainbow appear in the sky opposite the sun after the rain is stopped? It represents the spectrum of seven colors. A Rainbow is a natural phenomenon that can attract our attention and influence our emotions. Remember our actions are influenced by many factors including our food habits, nature, thoughts, and colors. Colors have a meaningful impact on our emotions, thought processes, behaviors, and energy levels. It also reflects the personality of the users.

"Color is not a trivial matter; it shapes and affects the feelings, the moods, the

thoughts, and the emotions of the people who are in its presence."- Faber Birren:

But how can you know which color is favorable and which can be avoided? The secret is there in the compatibility of numbers relating to Moolanka & Bhagyanka. For a better understanding let us see the compatibility chart.

Number	Friends	Non-Friends	Neutral
1	9,2,5,3,6,1	8	4,7
2	1,5,3,2	8,4,9	6,7
3	1,5,3,2,7*	6	4,8,9,7*
4	7,1,5,6,4*,8*	4*,8*,2,9	3
5	1,2,3,6,5	....	7,8,9,4
6	1,5,7,6	3	8,9,2,4
7	4,6,1,3,5	....	2,8,9,7
8	5,6,3,7,4*,8*	(4*,8*,)1,2,	9
9	1,5,3	4,2	6,7,8,9

Chart A

The friendly colors to the birth chart that are friendly with both Moolanka and Bhagyanka are considered lucky colors. The reverse is unlucky for the birth chart. There are 81 combinations of Moolanka and Bhagyanka, based on which lucky and unlucky colors are calculated. Before proceeding with the calculation of the lucky color for a birth chart, let me tell you the lucky color for each number starting from 1 to 9.

Number	Governing planet	Lucky color
1	Sun	Red, orange
2	Moon	White, blue
3	Jupiter	Yellow
4	Rahu	Grey, greyish-black
5	Mercury	Green
6	Venus	White, light blue, indigo
7	Ketu	Smokey brown, greyish green, green
8	Saturn	Dark blue, black
9	Mars	Red

Chart B

Significance of the Color in Numerology:

- Red is a vibrant color that symbolizes leadership, passion, and confidence to achieve goals.

- **Orange represents** creativity, harmony, and emotional balance,

- **Yellow is a color of** joy, optimism, and intellectual clarity.

- **Grey** (the combinations of black + white) makes you stable, confident, successful, rational, and sensible.

- **Green** is a symbol of rebirth, growth, peace, prosperity, fertility, cheerfulness and helping nature.

- **Indigo** (the combinations of blue +violet) is a color of wisdom, a sense of self-integrity.

- **Smokey brown** represents resilience, stability, strength, and dependability.

- **Black is a symbol of** power, authority, knowledge, and integrity.

- **White is a color of** calmness, spirituality, good luck, and fortune.

- **Blue** represents freedom, adaptability, and communication.

Let me show you how to calculate the lucky color of a birth chart. You know that Moolanka and Bhagyanka are two important elements in a numeroscope. Most of the predictions are being made based on these two numbers.

For example, take the date of birth of Janson(male) as 19.02.2015

	9	22
3	5	
	11	

M-1, B-2 K-3

- For 1 friendly number are 9,2,5,3,6,1 and

- For 2 they are 1,5,3,2.

- Nonfriends are 8 for Moolanka 1

- 8,4,9 are nonfriends for Bhagyanka 2.

- Common friends for both M-B are 1,2,3,5

- Nonfriends are 8,4,9.

- Neutral numbers are 4,7 for 1

- 6,7 neutral number for 2.

- The neutral number 7 is common for both.

Now we got 1,2,3,5 as common friends and 7 as neutral for both the M & B.

Now see the colors chart (**chart B).** What are the lucky colors for 1,2,3,5? These are **red, white, blue, yellow, and green.** Number 7 is a neutral number we can consider **Smokey brown, and greyish green** as a favorable color. **The lucky colors of Janson are red, white, blue, yellow, and green.**

Then which are unlucky color for Janson? These are **indigo, light blue, and black** to be avoided.

Anti-planet birth chart:

The antiplanets in numerology are **3-6, 1-8, and 2-8**. When anti-planets are placed in a birth chart as M-B, precautions must be taken for the upliftment of numbers and selection of colors.

For example, DOB of N-12.06.2013(Male)

		22
33	5	
8	11	6

M-3, B-6 K-5

In this birth chart,

- Friendly numbers for 3 are 1,5,3,2,7, and 6 are 1,5,7,6.

- Neutral numbers for 3 are 4,8,9,7 and for 6 are 8,9,2,4

- Common friends are 1,5,7

Now you can select the colors belonging to 1,5, and 7 for the birth chart. No favorable color for anti-planets be selected.

How can you use color in your favor?

Color represents many things in our life. Color selection speaks about the personality, mindset, emotions, etc. It gives an identity to your attire if you choose the right color for the right occasion. It is immaterial whether you are rich or poor, your choice of color is key to your success. For better mood and success, intelligent use of color in your daily life is important. Where can you use the color?

- Clothing.

- Interior decoration of your home.

- Vehicle you use.

- Gadgets.

- Writing tools(physical).

Summary:

This chapter explains how color plays a pivotal role in shaping our emotions, actions, and personality. Colors like those seen in a rainbow, are not merely visual experiences but influential factors in our lives. These colors influence our moods, thoughts, and energy levels, and even reflect our personalities. According to numerology, selecting favorable colors based on the compatibility between Moolanka (birth number) and Bhagyanka (destiny number) can enhance one's luck and success.

A detailed compatibility chart illustrates how different numbers relate to one another as friends, non-friends, or neutral. Furthermore, the chapter outlines the lucky colors associated with each number, governed by planets like the Sun, Moon, and Saturn. For instance, red symbolizes leadership, while green signifies growth and prosperity. By analyzing Moolanka and Bhagyanka, individuals can determine their lucky colors and avoid those unfavorable colors, enhancing both personal and professional success. The chapter emphasizes how the intelligent use of color in daily life—from clothing to interior design—can significantly impact mood, identity, and success. Ultimately, color is a powerful, often overlooked tool that can be strategically used for personal upliftment.

Chapter Five

NUMBERS SPEAK THE PROFESSIONS

"Numerology is the science of numbers that reveals the hidden meaning behind our lives." - Unknown

As you know every number is special in numerology. Each number speaks about professions. Each number is affiliated with a planet, and the professions are detected as per the nature of the planets. Let us talk about the professions relating to the planets.

1(Sun):

One is king. It can perform the best in any profession. The most preferably in a profession with authority, luxury, glamour, power, and freedom. It also represents fire. The professions may be administrative posts (IAS, IPS, CEO), politics, army, commander, or acting on the silver screen. Further one can get a job in steel plants, aluminium plants, and any industry where fire is used as a principal element.

2(Moon):

The moon represents water and mother. The professions for the number 2 can be milk production units, water treatment, water bottling plants, navy, soft drink, salt, coral, pearls, perfumes, nursing, farming, mother and child care products, cooking, etc.

3(Jupiter):

The Jupiter represents knowledge. Can you say who imparts knowledge and where is the knowledge? You know it. It is the education sector. The education sector is riched in teachers, mentors, trainers, councilors, spiritual leaders, yoga gurus, etc. One can be a promoter or belong to a teaching community. One can choose the noble professions like **healing, occult,** yoga, spiritual teaching, and doctors relating to number 3.

4(Rahu):

Rahu is a symbol of discipline and organization. The people having number 4 as Moolanka can choose any profession in law and judiciary. They may be judge and lawyers. The sales and marketing sectors may also suit them and rise to a decision-making process in the company. The service in the police and army may also suit them.

5(Mercury):

The Mercury is for any job or profession preferably a sitting one. The best profession for number 5 may be banking, financial sectors, computer applications, real estate sectors, investors in property, property dealers, etc.

6(Venus):

Venus for any profession with glamor and luxury. The best-suited professions are hotel industries, readymade garments, media, tour & travel, cosmetics & jewellery, spa and saloon, bar and restaurant, liquor sectors, casino, acting, dancing and singing, etc.

7(Ketu):

Ketu represents wisdom. **Occult, teaching,** scientific research(scientists), healing, and doctors, are the professions suggested for Ketu. Further detective investigations sectors like CBI, raw, FIA, CIA, and Mossad can be suitable for number 7.

8(Saturn):

Saturn represents discipline and justice. The law sector can be a suitable profession for people with 8 as Moolanka. The other sectors associated with 8 are leather, iron, cement, bricks, sanitary appliances, hardware, coals, etc.

9(Mars):

Mars is a commander and warrior. The professions suitable for 9 are in the army, police, teaching, healing, medicines, surgery, plywood, metal, electronic goods, NGO, etc.

The above professions suggested are indicative. The actual prediction can be made from the numeroscope. The next chapter can shed more light on this subject.

Summary:

In numerology, each number is linked to specific professions, guided by the influence of its governing planet. Number 1 (Sun) thrives in authoritative roles like politics, administration, and industries relating to the fire element. Number 2 (Moon) excels in professions related to water, motherhood, and care, such as nursing or farming. Jupiter (3) leads to education, healing, and spiritual professions, while Rahu (4) favors law, sales, and disciplined roles. Mercury (5) suits banking and real estate, Venus (6) glamor and luxury, and Ketu (7) wisdom and investigation. Saturn (8) excels in professions in discipline and justice, and Mars (9) in military and medical fields. These suggestions guide one toward career success.

Chapter Six

DETECTION OF PROFESSIONS FROM NUMEROSCOPE

"Numerology can provide insights into our relationships, career paths, and personal challenges." - Unknown

Earning for yourself and your family is key to existence. You might have heard the concept of "**struggle for existence and survival of the fittest**" a core principle of Charles Darwin's theory of evolution by natural selection. This principle is now more or less applied to human existence. In the fast-changing world, the rich are becoming richer, and the poor are becoming poorer. Why such an unbalancing scenario for the most talented creations of the universe? Because of the mobilization of resources at the right time for the right cause by the riches.

The different resources we have identified for our progress include human resources. You are a resource of knowledge and power but unaware of it. Resource means financial gain. You will get more if you can identify your core area of excellence relating to your profession, business, etc. How can you know your core area of preference for financial well-being? Which profession can earn your name, fame, and money? It can be known from your numeroscope and the detection of profession.

How do you detect your profession?

I have discussed earlier, that Moolanka, Bhagyanka, and Kua numbers are very important for a numeroscope. When we talk about the detection of a profession from a particular birth chart Moolanka is considered very important. Next comes Bhagyanka. The compatibility of Moolanka and Bhagyanka for detecting a profession is important. If Moolanka and Bhagyanka are anti numbers then no profession can be detected either of two. Any other profession can be detected out of the other numbers available in the chart. However, the opposite number of Moolanka and Bhagyanka can be considered for detecting a profession.

Anti-M-B

M	B
1	8
2	8
8	2
3	6
6	3
8	1

Opposite M-B

M	B
4	2
2	4
4	9
9	4
9	9
7	7

For the right prediction of the professions let me show you some numeroscopes.

4	9	22
3		7
	11	66

M-4 C-2 K-6

This numeroscope belongs to a very famous coach. In this birth chart, M-4 predicts marketing as a profession. In his early phase, he was working on a marketing farm, and his name and fame. Later, he started his career as an education coach for numbers 3 & 7. As both the numbers lean toward occult and teaching, the person is a famous numerologist and Vastu Coach.

Take another example,

Tapan: DOB-25.09.1981

	99	2
	5	7
88	11	

M-7, B-8 K-1

In this instance case Tapan could have opted for a profession like **Occult, teaching,** scientific research(scientists), healing, or the profession for number 8. But he has not preferred either of the two. He did his Post Graduation in economics and found his luck in the banking sector which is the profession of 5. Now he is acting as bank manager in a public sector bank in India. Here is a point to note education is another factor for detecting the profession. If he had done law, the judicial sector would have been best for him, as 88 is the best suited for the law sector. The teaching profession is another area that can have suited him.

Sachin Tendulkar: DOB-24.4.1973

44	9	2
33		7
	1	6

M-6 B-3 K-9

Sachin Tendulkar is one of the best cricketers in the world. His Moolanka is 6 and Bhagyanka is 3. Both M & B are anti-numbers. Hence, he has not chosen any profession of M or B, which was the right decision. He has two lines complete; one is 4, 9, 2 horizontal lines called a mental plane and another is 2,7,6 the vertical plane. The plane is a line of action-takers and risk-takers. This line is for physical sports. Cricket is a physical sport. Numerologically Sachin's birth chart is one of the brightest examples.

What are important things to consider when detecting one's profession?

- Moolanka or Psychic number

- Bhagyanka or lifepath number

- If the above numbers are anti then avoid the profession of both the numbers.

- No professions should be advised against the missing numbers.

- Educational qualification to be taken into consideration while detecting a profession.

Detection of the profession from the birth chart depends on different numbers and factors. Unless you study it deeply you can't detect the profession.

Summary:

Detecting one's profession through numerology involves understanding the roles of Moolanka (birth number), Bhagyanka (life path number), and other numbers. The compatibility of Moolanka and Bhagyanka, guides us toward detecting the ideal profession for financial success and personal fulfillment. If the numbers are anti to each other, their related professions should be avoided, and alternate professions from other favorable numbers can be chosen. While detecting profession the role of education should be given importance in this process. By studying a birth chart deeply, one can uncover the most promising profession, ensuring prosperity and balance in life.

Chapter Seven

BIG ARROW AND SMALL ARROW

"Numerology can help us understand ourselves and our purpose in life." - Unknown

Recall the Lo-Shu Grid and its structure. I have told you that all the predictions, future paths, and detection of the profession are made on the very foundation of the Lo-Shu Grid structure. Let me once again show you the grid for a proper understanding of this topic.

4	9	3
3	5	7
8	1	6

As you know the above grid contains three vertical, three horizontal, and two diagonal lines. It has been discussed in chapter 2.

BIG ARROW:

Vertical arrow: ↑-4,3,8:

The characteristics of the numbers may differ but when united they can act differently. All three numbers can have different equations.

- The people having this line are likely to be big planners, which means they do the work with proper planning and execute them properly.

- They are shrewd and cunning. They can manage things in their favor smartly. This line or arrow is best suited for politics.

↑9,1,5:

- The people who have this vertical line in their birth charts are decision-makers and fighters.

- They can make the right decisions at the right time without hurriedly.

- They are also fighters and resilient people. They remain focused on their objectives and can bounce back smartly.

↑**2,7,6:**

- The people who are blessed with this vertical line are good opportunists.

- They can settle things in their favor.

- Always remain in readiness to grab opportunities.

- They are good for outdoor games and sports.

Horizontal Arrow: →

There are three horizontal lines in the Loshu Grid.

→**4,9,2:**

- The people with such a line are very intellectual.

- They can remember things easily.

- They can achieve success with their intellectual integrity and sharp memory.

→**3,5,7:**

- The people with such a line in their birth chart have a golden heart means very soft-hearted. They can't see the sufferings of others. They are compassionate.

- They are emotional. The emotion lands them in cheating and foolishness. They are emotionally black males and cheat in love.

- They are religious, God-loving, and spiritual in heart.

- They are creative artists, who love music and the occult.

→ 8,1,6:

- This is called the arrow of prosperity.

- They are very practical in their approach and outlook.

- They are logical and prosperous. Analytical minds make them rich and make the right financial decisions.

Diagonal arrows: ↗: ↘

↗ 4,5,6:

It is a symbol of aggression. The people with this line are destined to become successful in their lives. They are aggressive but at the same time balanced. They are normally rich and financially very strong.

They are very focused and have patience. Never lost their objective despite setbacks. Wait for the right time to act. **Heat the iron when it is hot proverb** is suited for them. A great thing for them is they built homes early in their life.

SMALL ARROW:

A small arrow means the entire line containing three numbers is not complete.

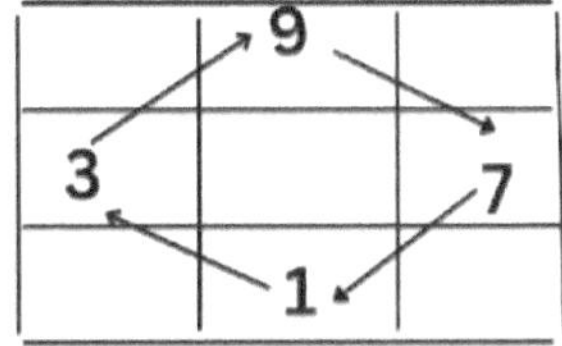

↘ **9,7:** The two numbers are responsible for keeping the person balanced in life during difficult situations. 9 is a fighter planet and 7 is the symbol of wisdom. The wisdom keeps the fighter calm and quiet as the situation demands. When you are in a difficult situation it is wise to keep silent irrespective of your social status and wellbeing.

↙**7,1:** This combination speaks about deep learning and research. The people with these lines often do research in the field of interest.

They are highly educated and understand things first by self-research.

↖1, 3: The people are intelligent, spiritual, and knowledgeable. They are very clear about the concept of the things they prefer.

↗3,9: The birth chart having 3&9 is litigant and arrogant. They never compromise even for small things which lands them in complicated lawsuits. The egoistic nature of the people makes them unhappy. They never admit their faults.

Summary:

The birth chart reveals key insights into a person's traits and potential professions. The vertical, horizontal, and diagonal arrows present in the birth chart speak the personality of an individual. Vertical arrows highlight planners, decision-makers, and opportunists, while horizontal lines reflect intellectuals, compassionate souls, and prosperous individuals. Diagonal arrows signify success through aggression, patience, or research. Small arrows, where lines are incomplete, hint at a person's ability to balance wisdom and strength or focus on deep learning. The grid serves as a foundation for understanding one's nature and guiding professional choices, making it an essential tool in numerology for self-awareness and career alignment.

CONCLUSION

Numerology is not just an ancient science; it is a powerful tool that can shape your career, destiny, and life. This book, *Numerology for Career Guidance*, explains the mystical relationship between numbers and our professional success. It has made us understand how our birth numbers, Moolanka (birth number), Bhagyanka (life path number), and other numbers of our birth chart form the foundation of our career choices, and how they interact to reveal our true potential.

The journey through this book has been more than just learning numerology—it's about understanding yourself on a profound level. No matter whether you're a student, a professional, or someone seeking change in your career path, numerology provides a roadmap for discovering your strengths, recognizing your weaknesses, and aligning your career with the energies that are most favorable for you.

The Role of Numbers in Your Career

The moment you were born, numbers governed your life, even if you weren't aware of it. The

Moolanka, Bhagyanka, and other numbers in your birth chart are intricately linked to your personality, abilities, and destiny. Each number carries a specific vibrational energy, and these vibrations resonate with the core of who you are. In this book, we have carefully examined how these numbers influence your professional life, guiding you toward careers that are most suited to your inherent traits.

Each number is also connected to a planet, and just like the planets influence various aspects of life in astrology, the numbers affect our career choices. The Sun (1) represents leadership and authority, making careers in politics, administration, and industries involving fire elements ideal. The Moon (2) governs nurturing roles such as nursing, farming, and water-related professions. Each planet has its own influence, guiding the choice of profession for individuals associated with its number.

But it's not just about finding the right profession based on your birth number. This book teaches you how to harmonize the energies of different numbers, helping you avoid professions that may not align with your destiny. The compatibility of your Moolanka and Bhagyanka plays a crucial role in determining whether a career path will bring you success or frustration. For example, if your Moolanka and Bhagyanka are incompatible, pursuing a career related to either number could result in challenges, which can be avoided by selecting professions linked to more favorable numbers in your chart.

The Lo-Shu Grid: The Foundation of Your Numeroscope

The Lo-Shu Grid, also known as the Laxmi Yantra, is the heart of numerology, providing a comprehensive view of your life, personality, and career path. This ancient 3x3 grid holds the key to unlocking your professional success. By analyzing the numbers in your grid, you can identify your strengths, weaknesses, and areas of opportunity.

The vertical, horizontal, and diagonal arrows within the Lo-Shu Grid offer insight into different aspects of your personality. For instance, those with vertical line 4, 3, and 8 are known for their strategic planning abilities, making them suitable for roles in politics and leadership. The vertical line of 9, 1, and 5 reveals decision-makers and resilient individuals who excel in challenging professions. Horizontal lines, such as 4, 9, and 2, indicate intellectual strength, while 3, 5, and 7 signify a compassionate and creative soul—ideal for artistic and spiritual professions.

The diagonal lines in the grid provide additional depth to the analysis, revealing traits such as aggression, patience, and focus, all of which play significant roles in shaping career choices. And for those whose birth charts have incomplete lines, or "small arrows," the grid reveals areas that need balance, allowing them to focus on self-improvement and achieving greater success in their careers.

This structured approach, using the Lo-Shu Grid, forms the backbone of your Numeroscope. By studying it deeply, you can align yourself with the energies that bring prosperity, growth, and fulfillment to your professional journey.

The Power of Compatibility and Color in Career Success

As we explored the compatibility of numbers in this book, we learned that just like human relationships, numbers too can be friendly, neutral, or in conflict with one another. This compatibility extends to personal and professional relationships, which can determine how well you work with others and whether you'll thrive in specific environments.

For example, number 1, representing the Sun, is closely aligned with 9 (Mars) and 2 (Moon), but clashes with 8 (Saturn). By understanding these interactions, you can avoid conflicts and harness the power of favorable numbers in your life and career. This knowledge is crucial when choosing business partners, collaborators, or even selecting a life partner who complements your numbers.

In addition to number compatibility, color plays a pivotal role in enhancing your success. Each number is associated with specific colors, and by using these colors strategically in your environment, attire, and daily life, you can boost your luck and productivity. Red, for instance, symbolizes leadership and is linked to the Sun, while green promotes growth and prosperity, representing Mercury. The understanding of color and its connection to numerology is a powerful tool that can help you harness the right energies for success.

Detecting Your Profession: The Path to Success

One of the core purposes of this book has been to guide you toward discovering your ideal profession through numerology. The process of detecting your profession is complicated but highly rewarding. It involves understanding the interplay between your Moolanka, Bhagyanka, and other key numbers, as well as considering your educational background and personal interests.

By analyzing your birth chart and studying your Numeroscope, you can identify the professions most suited to your natural talents and strengths. For example, a person with Moolanka 4 and Bhagyanka 9 may excel in marketing and education, while someone with Moolanka 7 and Bhagyanka 8 may find success in scientific research, healing, or the judicial sector.

Education plays an important role in this process, as it can open doors to professions that may not seem immediately obvious from your numbers. As we saw in the case of Tapan, whose Moolanka 7 and Bhagyanka 8 indicated potential in law or teaching, his decision to pursue a career in banking (linked to number 5) was influenced by his education in economics. This illustrates how numerology can guide you, but personal choices and education also play a significant role in shaping your career.

Unlocking Your True Potential

At its core, numerology is about self-discovery. It is a journey of understanding who you are, what you are capable of, and how you can align your life with the energies that support your growth and success. This book has taken you through the intricate process of calculating and analyzing your numbers, using the Lo-Shu Grid. It also empowers you to decode your strengths and weaknesses and provides practical guidance on how to choose the right career.

The knowledge you've gained from this book equips you to not only understand yourself but also to help others on their journey. Whether it's creating Numeroscopes for friends and family or guiding them toward the right career path, numerology offers endless possibilities for personal and professional development.

In conclusion, ***Numerology for Career Guidance*** is more than just a book—it's a roadmap to success. By embracing the wisdom of numbers and aligning your life with their vibrations, you can unlock hidden opportunities, overcome challenges, and create a career that brings you fulfillment, prosperity, and happiness. The numbers are always speaking to you; now you have the tools to listen and act. Let this book be your guide as you continue your journey toward unlocking your destiny through the power of numerology.

DISCLAIMER

The information provided in this book, *Numerology for Career Guidance*, is intended for educational and entertainment purposes only. Numerology is a metaphysical practice and should not be considered a definitive or scientific method for career decisions. While numerological insights can offer unique perspectives and reflections on one's career potential, personal growth, and life path, they are not substitutes for professional advice or practical decision-making.

Readers are encouraged to use the information as a complementary tool in their personal development. Decisions regarding education, career, and finances should be made after careful consideration and consultation with qualified professionals, such as career counselors, financial advisors, or industry experts.

The author and publisher disclaim any responsibility or liability for any actions or decisions taken based on the contents of this book. Numerology is subjective and may vary in interpretation; therefore, results and insights may differ for each individual.

By reading this book, you acknowledge that you are solely responsible for your career choices and the outcomes thereof.

●★✪★●

MAY I ASK YOU FOR A SMALL FAVOR?

At the outset, I want to give a big thanks for taking out time to read this book. You could have chosen any other book, but you chose mine, and I totally appreciate this.

I hope you got at least a few actionable insights that will have a positive impact on your day-to-day life.

Can I ask for 30 seconds more of your time?

I would love it if you could leave a review about the book. Reviews may not matter to big-name authors; but they're a tremendous help for authors like me, who don't have many followers. They help me grow my readership by encouraging folks to take a chance on my books.

To put it straight, reviews are the lifeblood of any author. I feel this book *Numerology for Career Guidance*, shall enrich you with some actionable steps.

Please leave your review by visiting the "**Review Section** "of this book's page on this platform.

It will just take less than a minute of your time, but will tremendously help me to reach out to more people, so please leave your review.

Thanks for your support of my work. And I would love to see your review.